STEVEN FROMHOLZ
NEW AND SELECTED POEMS

STEVEN FROMHOLZ
NEW AND SELECTED POEMS

TCU PRESS
FORT WORTH, TEXAS

TCU TEXAS POETS LAUREATE SERIES

Library of Congress Cataloging-in-Publication Data

Fromholz, Steven.
  [Poems. Selections]
  New and selected poems / Steven Fromholz.
      p. cm. -- (TCU Texas poets laureate series)
  ISBN-13: 978-0-87565-359-4 (cloth : alk. paper)
  ISBN-10: 0-87565-359-6
  1. Texas--Poetry. I. Title.

PS3606.R63A6 2007
811'.6--dc22

                                    2007034188

    This book is made possible by a generous Vision in Action grant from TCU.
    Book design by Tom Martens at fusion29. www.fusion29.com

DEDICATION
THIS BOOK OF POETRY IS DEDICATED TO MY SISTER,
ANGELA BLAIR, WITHOUT WHOSE NOMINATION
OF ME FOR POET LAUREATE OF TEXAS, NONE OF THIS
WOULD HAVE TRANSPIRED.

table of contents

INTRODUCTION

Most Texas Poets Laureate are known only for the poems they have written—and
perhaps for essays in poetic criticism—but Steven Fromholz is known for much
more than his verses. He wrote "I'd Have to Be Crazy," recorded by Willie Nelson,
which garnered him two platinum records, and his three-part tribute to Bosque
County, *The Texas Trilogy*, is one of the great classics of Texas music. Steven
Fromholz, the actor, has appeared in several movies, including the Peter Fonda
film *Outlaw Blues*, the Willie Nelson-Kris Kristofferson vehicles *Songwriter* and
Cloak and Dagger, and co-starred in Andy Anderson's *Positive ID*. His theatre work
includes *The Night Hank Williams Died*, *Sweeney Todd*, *The Immigrant*, *A Christmas
Carol*, *A Little Night Music*, and starring as the redoubtable Tevye in *Fiddler On
the Roof*.

Among my souvenirs is a clipping from the *Denton Record-Chronicle*
telling how Steve Fromholz scored the winning goal in a basketball game between
Denton High and one of its chief rivals. Although born in Temple, Steven grew
up in Kopperl, Texas, and later Denton, where he attended high school and the
University of North Texas. I can't claim that I know Steven Fromholz, but I used
to join him and a bunch of singers and guitarists when I would take my trusty
Stella Guitar to Stan Alexander's house once a week to try and learn to pick
"The Wildwood Flower."

Stan Alexander, one of the finest singers and pickers in Texas, was on
the English Faculty of UNT (then North Texas State University) and his weekly
gatherings included a number of musically inclined students and the unmusical
me. Among the students were Steven Fromholz, Michael Martin Murphy, B.W.
Stevenson, and the other half-dozen who did not become famous. Even the great

chronicler of American country music, Bill Malone, got his early lessons from Stan and Company.

After leaving UNT, Steven served in the navy and thereafter teamed up with Dan McCrimmon in Colorado, to form Frummox, a duo that developed a devoted cult following. When the pair went separate ways, Steven toured with Stephen Stills and eventually became a solo act. His best-known work is his celebrated *Texas Trilogy*, which narrates life in Kopperl, Bosque County, Texas. The three parts of the song, "Daybreak," "Trainride," and "Bosque County Romance," have been recorded by Fromholz himself on his album *Frummox: Here to There* and also by Lyle Lovett on his CD *Step Inside This House*, Lovett's tribute to his most admired songwriters. Fromholz and Don Toner, of Austin, co-authored a stage play, *Bosque County Romance*, based on the song.

Author Craig Hillis and Photographer Bruce Jordan published *Texas Trilogy: Life In A Small Texas Town* in 2002 (University of Texas Press) using Fromholz' song, *Texas Trilogy*, as their inspiration. Fromholz himself released his first book *Texas Trilogy* in August, 2007 (Esteban Press), which presents the narrative, never before published family pictures, an essay by the author on growing up in Kopperl, Texas, and a foreword by friend and author, Bud Shrake.

Steven's poetry appears in his songs and in the pure poems that he has written over many years. His lyrical "I Walked with My Daughter Today" was written not long after he got out of the navy in 1968. Even then, almost forty years ago, he captured in verse what many fathers feel when talking and walking with a child. The last stanza is:

I walked with my daughter today.

Chewing gum and baby's breath

Filled my face and she shouted "gum"

And laughed as she hugged my neck.

When we crossed the last street

I walked with my daughter today

And for a short time

I was dragon slayer to a princess.

This poignant poem about a daughter was followed five or six years later by "Here's to My Old Man," wherein the poet reflects on his father, now long gone. In the final stanza, he regrets that he never knew his father after he, himself, became an adult.

But as a man I've one regret

He never shook an older hand

So fill your cups in calm respect.

Here's to my old man.

Some of Fromholz' poems are song lyrics. Song/poems like "High Country Caravan," "The Last Livin' Outlaw," and "Where Are They All Now" are, like his poetry, evocative of nature, memories of the past, and plans for the future. In "Where Are They All Now," he recaptures a long lost childhood and the poem/song ends:

Where are they all now?

Can you tell me?

Were they really real?

Have you seen them?

Where are they all now?

Both the songs and poems of Steven Fromholz tell of a life that began with "bikes and trikes and kites and trees" and progressed through fatherhood and many days and nights spent on the road, the people he's met, and the friends he's made along the way. As a poet, he is as well worth reading as he is a singer worth hearing. His masterwork, to date, is the great song *Trilogy* but there are poems in this volume that are equally as fine.

Toward the end of this volume, he summarizes much of what he's seen and done in a poem he titles "Being Had By The Fun." The refrain line, "being had by the fun" recaptures much of Steven's life. Here are a few of the stanzas that catch the spirit of what it means to be Steven Fromholz:

> I still have some friends
> Who are facing dead ends
> Being had by the fun.
>
> Ah, the nights spent in jail
> Waiting on bail
> Being had by the fun.
>
> Oh, the pall we have carried
> For the friends we have buried
> Who got had by the fun.

Steven Fromholz has lived a full and interesting life for sixty-two years. He was inducted into the Texas Music Hall of Fame in March 2003 and in April of the same year suffered a massive stroke. Always the eternal optimist, he summarizes the stroke incident as, "it's not so much a coming back as it is a going on!" He's again performing, guiding whitewater river trips, trail riding, writing music, and, of course, writing the poetry that caused the Texas State Legislature to name him Poet Laureate of Texas for 2007.

THE MAN WITH THE BIG HAT

In a bar in Arizona, on a sultry summer day,
A cowboy came in off the road just to pass the time away.
He pulled a stool up to the bar, pushed his hat back on his head.
I listened to the stories told, to the words the cowboy said, he said,

"I can tell you stories 'bout the Indians on the plains,
Talk about Wells Fargo and the comin' of the trains.
Talk about the slaughter of the buffalo that roamed.
Tell of all the settlers come out lookin' for a home.

"Now the man with the big hat is buyin'.
Drink up while the drinkin' is free.
Drink up to the cowboys a'dead or a'dyin;
Drink to my compadres and me. Drink to my compadres and me."

Well, his shirt was brown and faded and his hat was wide and black.
And the pants that once were blue were grey and had a pocket
    gone in back.
He had a finger missin' from the hand that rolled a smoke
He smiled and talked of cowboys, but you knew it weren't no joke.

He said, "I've seen a day so hot your pony could not stand,
And if your water bag was dry don't count upon the land.
And winters, I've seen winters when your boots froze in the snow,
And your only thought was leavin' but you had no place to go."

He rested easy at the bar, his foot upon the rail,
And laughed and talked of times he'd had while livin' on the trail.
The silence never broken as the words poured from his lips.
As quiet as the .45 he carried on his hip.

He said, "I rode the cattle drives from here to San Antone;
Ten days in the saddle and weary to the bone.
I've rode from here to Wichita without a woman's smile,
And the fire where I cooked my beans was the only light for miles."

He rolled another cigarette as he walked toward the door.
I heard his spurs a'jinglin' as his boot heels hit the floor.
He loosened up his belt a notch, pulled his hat down on his head.
Turned to say goodbye to me and this is what he said,

"Now the high lines chase the highways and the fences
   close the range,
And to see a workin' cowboy is a sight that's mighty strange.
A cowboy's life was lonely and his lot was not the best,
But if it wasn't for the life he lived there wouldn't be no West.

"Now the man with the big hat is buyin'.
Drink up while the drinkin' is free.
Drink up to the cowboys a'dead or a'dyin;
Drink to my compadres and me. Drink to my compadres and me."

new orleans fantasy

He came by about six and rang the bell.
I went to the door and helped him in.
Old but not bent, wrinkled but not withered.
I placed the ashtray on his left, the wine on his right
And told him this.
A candle burned brightly behind his grey-streaked head
And his cigar glowed as a cat's eye
As we each sat in silence,
Waiting for the other to begin.

"We will pass away the night?"
"As you wish," I replied.
I did not know why he came but was elated to see him once more.
The candle flickered as the unseen wind moved through my room.
"We will talk of my life and I will go as I came."
He spoke on through the night
And I listened, never moving
Or taking my weary eyes from his face,
In the circle of candlelight.

He talked of childhood;
Life as a young man;
His wife and children,
All passed before him.
He told me of his loneliness
As an old man grew even older.
The house, the voices, footsteps,
Laughter, tears, and God.
A shorter candle still shone bright.

The old man's voice was strong,
Still sounding
As the first traces of the oncoming day
Showed themselves
Through the half-shuttered window glass.
"I see the sun is rising," he said.
"How can a blind man see?" I thought.
The candle was cold.

TO THEODORE

If silken swift your time is telling,
Talking bares your future seeing,
Scritchy, scratchy; running at your feet.
Soft, smooth hands you notice quickly,
Lonely is a word well meaning,
Love, behind the glass door, bittersweet.

When flannel, rats, and garbage cans
And gentlemanly cowboys ride
And barrel-chested doubles, these you see,
The woman-man spreads slow her word
And white ants speak with human tongue
Fingerless musicians play for thee.

If mysteries of night entice you,
Begging not to be remembered,
Then you ride the steed with golden horn.
If cats and waxen figurines
Are well known objects of late hours,
Then you know the Man of the Unicorn.

NEW ATTITUDE

New attitude, new day, same people.
Fresh smiles after washing away
Yesterday's grimness with last night's tears.
Why not? If you let yourself,
You can be anything, anything
. . . everything to one who believes.

Kids come laughin' in and flip out
Because the guitar glows in the dark light.
"Advits" freak out because God doesn't.
If they only knew that the light
Has to be inside
. . . and Jesus called it "Faith."

Where does one get his share of faith
To turn on God? Maybe from you?
Living around and in a gentle person
Can't warm one and if in becoming you,
Becoming anything,
It should be gentle.

Such a soft word "Gentle."
Gentle can be touched,
Tasted, smelled, kissed, seen, and loved,
And if something can't be loved,
I'm not sure
What good It is.

DOUBLE TROUBLE

Rambling on and on and on,
I sit here wondering.
Why minds have heads
And why are spirits always wrapped
As yesterday's newspaper?

It is forever, since six years past,
When I last sat and rambled.
Situations, like buzzards, rise
And circle, circle, circle.
The feast of the same.

And change, changes, changing
Control of situations, as of buzzards,
Is multiplied by two.
Double trouble
Troubles the mind of a man.

I WALKED WITH MY DAUGHTER TODAY

I walked with my daughter today,
And for a short time
I felt like a giant.
Striding slowly across the city with my small friend,
Asking and answering each other's questions
About blue Fords
And how's your arm,
And trucks that spin on the back,
And are you tired of walking?
Yep!

I walked with my daughter today
And the newness of her everything amazed me
And I was envious.
She heard the bird that only chirped
Because I wasn't listening and she laughed.
She saw an auto hydraulically lifted into the air
And her blue eyes went wide.
She cried when we had to leave
Her pretty fish in the aquarium
And only left at all on promise of ice cream.

I walked with my daughter today
Down darkening Denver winter streets,
Looking at shadows
Where leaves used to be
And shivering against the wind.
Our hot fudge turned to simple strawberry
Because ice cream parlors sometimes
Close at four-thirty.
But, warmth and laughter and "Isn't she cute?"
Loved an afternoon into evening.

I walked with my daughter today.
Chewing gum and baby's breath
Filled my face and she shouted "gum"
And laughed,
And I shouted "gum"
And laughed as she hugged my neck.
When we crossed the last street
I walked with my daughter today
And for a short time
I was dragon slayer to a princess.

LIFE SONG

Sing tenderly
Of life emerging from life.
A waiting, breathless, bodyless child
Begins in a breathless, waiting body
From loving to loving,
Begins.

Sing urgently,
Of urgency of entrance of child
Into air and light and pain
In the semi-awareness of not knowing
Existence of self
Only hunger and cold are immediate.

Sing sadly
In the fleeting happiness of childhood.
The backwardness of body leading mind;
The impossible paradox of learning love
And living hate;
The realization of life begins.

Sing wondrously of love,
Love mate found, heart lost.
But, in losing, becoming filled
With myriad memories.
Guard dearly your dearest, lest one destroy one.
For young, all love is immediate.

Sing swiftly
In rushing years,
Pushing youth under
And behind drying flesh.
A weary eye,
Views with shy fear

The inevitable approach of
An irrevocable destiny
Of all who, once long ago,
Had no choice.
And now a vigil, wait, anticipation,
Filled with unwelcome impatience begins.

Sing softly
Of a lyrical loveliness
So deftly desecrated
By the fatal foot of man
Let all begin
Immediately.

Proposal No. 1

In her room I lay in grey contemplation
Of a day and my position in same.
Riding the broomstick dreams of rogues out of rhythm,
And cowboys out of time;
Standing vacantly in empty corrals,
Where prairies once were.
Searching the biting right angles of a metric world
For one long, slow, lingering curve,
Beginning at me
And be it long enough,
Ending at me.

I have danced with fools,
And felt fit in the rankless wanderings of gypsies;
The day-by-day ones.
And yet, enough!
My heart does not cry,
And should the present become the past in failure,
I pray my heart should stand as a mountain,
That I might cling to its ledges against those
Who would cast down stones,
To crush what I believe to be
Honor and truth.

sonneT NO. 1

In my dreams,
Love is the burial of one king
Only to crown him anew
And likewise, he is all that is his
And he is good.

In his fairly held reign
Shall the harvest multiply
And on the smiles
Of the children
Shall the bitter winds turn their backs.

His fine wife
Shall be kind, just and lovely
And give to him sons and daughters
And patience.
His subjects, and his love, shall prosper.

A LITTLE RED BOOK and a ROSE

I used to have a Little Red Book
That was more of me
Than I am.
I can remember the dawns
That caught me tryin' my damndest
To paint a portrait of my soul
In that Little Red Book.

It was one of my secret things,
That Little Red Book,
And no one needed to know
Anything about it but me.
That's the way it was for days and days and days.
I was pretty close to happy
I had someone to talk to.

And then one day, as suddenly as a smile
She was sitting in the booth beside me.
No, not the one I shared a bed with,
(Not that I didn't want to);
No, she was the Lady of the Rose
Whom I laughed with.
I also cried with my Lady of the Rose.

With my Little Red Book in one hand
And my Rose in the other
We would talk for hours (when I could steal them)
Or moments when I could not
In booths, car seats, and benches,
But they were all flying carpets to a peaceful mind,
Even if just for the moment.

But a stupidly sunny Saturday came along
And I, with Little Red Book in hand was gone,
Leaving my legal bed better off empty,
And my Lady of the Rose behind
In a sad city that never knew me.
I lose myself now in a Big Black Book
But it's not a Little Red Book

With vinyl cover
And three rings.
There's paper and lines here,
But it's not the same.
It serves as a surface for my pen
And shows my words
But it doesn't really listen.

I miss my Little Red Book and its brother,
Who sits sad and unfinished in Arizona
Among other secret things I had to leave.
My Lady of the Rose has gone on
But I am lucky and have found another.
A Lady of the Rose
Is so, so, so rare.

Here's TO MY OLD Man

Yes, to the days we don't remember
All afar and nearly gone.
And to all the long December
Days he thought I'd never come.

In Texas, as a baby coming
Six months hence to start again
At tasks he must have then held sacred,
Not to mention fun, and then,

On Ashworth Road in Iowa
On icy days when doors were closed
A chase across a snowy mound
That sunlight freed and north wind froze.

There's fish alive in Minnesota
Just because we never went
To fish there, for the days were dollars;
Money earned was money spent.

But those in Texas took their turn
On Sundays when the time was free
To talk and wander, walk and wonder
What the day could then foresee.

Soon to Tennessee we headed.
When? I couldn't rightly say
The day we left or when we got there
Time was short; he'd dues to pay,

For things I've never even found out
What or why or when or who.
But days were short and tight and heavy
Can't explain what men will do.

There's days between of never knowing
Effort spent on neither side
And years gone by in cool forgetfulness
No need for alibis.

But as a man I've one regret
He never shook an older hand
So fill your cups in calm respect.
Here's to my old man.

FOR MY BROTHER AND ME

It's a lot like standing
Immediately in a very dark room.
It's not just dark
But rather blind and deaf.
No sensations.
You're pretty sure you can't talk
But your fear forces you
To total and complete silence.
Not just silence,
Nothing.

You don't move
Because you're sure
The room has no walls
On the inside;
Only on the outside.
"How did I get here," you think,
And the thought rips
At the edges of your mind
And rattles all you hold close
And you know.

Where's the light switch?
Is there a light switch?
Is there a light?
There's only whatever is inside of you,
Inside of whatever you are inside of.

Then, as simply as laughing,
A door, way off in the little bitty distance, opens.
A light, like living, pours in
And you can see you were right.
There were no walls,
And a little cat
With Suzanne in one hand
And a flat pick in the other,
Wearing St. Anne street boots says,
"Dynamite man, I'm Jamie Brockett."

HIGH COUNTRY caravan

The crystal gaze softness, unbroken the sunlight
And rainbows have died for the day.
A pine needle pillow of dreamed upon memories,
Walked over winds blown away.
Time doesn't enter my singular solitude,
Mysteries of night thoughts come begging to me,
Where lonely well meaning, is only allowable
Thoughts of my past bring my present to me.

I laugh at my lyrics, while singing with night birds,
The words only mess up the tune.
Count all the stars till I run out of numbers,
Find that I'm sleeping too soon.
Night is for laughing or walking a quiet path,
Lying in clover on top of a hill,
But I lay here dreaming of sailing on silver wings
Morning comes dancing and I'm dreaming still.

I'm off on a high country caravan,
Gone again,
Following the ones who went before.
Don't think that I'm going back again . . .
I couldn't stand the games of man
I just won't play at all no more.
Sit in the sunrise and search for the morning star
Fighting the sun to be seen.

Standing in springtime
And watching the trees working
Changing the dead leaves to green.
Daylight it decorates all that it falls upon
Everything 'round me it feels like my own.
Walking a straight path
From here over yonder ways,
Me feeling happy for once all alone.

I'm off on a high country caravan,
Where I've been
Is all a sin
I'd just as soon forget.
Can't see no reason to look behind,
I might find
Some of the kind I've seen before,
We've already met.

Down cross the valley
And on through the creek beds
My footprints are seen by the dove.
He flies on by me and calls to his love mate
The smile fits my face like a glove.
Out cross the gullies the going gets rougher now,
I turn loose my footsteps, they go where they will.
If you pass this way you might possibly find me there . . .
. . . Staring at God from the top of a hill.

THE LAST LIVIN' OUTLAW

You just might encounter his mangy old carcass
And he might look a million and he might look like hell,
In a beer joint in Beaumont or at Neiman Marcus,
His lawyer allows how he cleans up quite well.

He lives by his wits and his wiles and his ways,
He lives with his memories etched on his face,
He may live forever
And he may live for days.

He's the last livin' outlaw, he's the last rolling smoker,
Sees life kind of southpaw, he's a nocturnal joker.
His best friends are barmaids, he's a pawnbroker's pal.
Let's drink to the last livin' outlaw!

He knows all the back roads from here to Kentucky
From haulin' those lovely colitas and bales.
He was contraband careful, uncommonly lucky
'Til a judge replaced smuggling with two years in jail.

He's wise to the ways of turnpikes and diners,
From spending his days
In a red/white Freightliner,
From Tulsa to Memphis to North Carolina.

He's the last livin' outlaw; he's a sixties survivor
He's still got a quick draw, he's an old diesel driver.
He still loves the highway—it left him alive!
Let's roll with the last livin' outlaw!

He's a honky tonk hero and always a gentleman.
He's just a rake and the ladies are leaves.
He's been married once . . . has a daughter named Gwendolyn,
She sends him letters—he rarely receives.

He's a hit with the ladies, he can dance on a horse.
He doesn't fear fightin' but avoids it of course.
Well, he once loved his wife—
Probably loved mine and yours!

He's the last livin' outlaw, he's a Friday night dancer,
He'll soon be a grandpaw; he's a lifetime romancer.
The ladies all love him for the light in his eyes—
Let's drink to the last livin' outlaw!

A LIST OF LOVER'S QUESTIONS

Can you stand another broken heart?
Can you sing love's sad refrain?
Can you stop before the teardrops start?
Or are you gonna cry again?
Can you bet your heart and let it ride?
Live and love and let the fates decide?
Is the gamble worth the gain?
Is the pleasure worth the pain?
Is the rainbow worth the rain?

I was reading in the book of love
(Need a copy? Borrow mine.)
I found a list of lover's questions
And they numbered only nine.
But we all must know the answers
To be equal to the task
Before you lose yourself in love, my friend,
These are the questions you must ask.

Can you stand another broken heart?
Can you sing love's sad refrain?
Can you stop before the teardrops start?
Or are you gonna cry again?
Can you bet your heart and let it ride?
Live and love and let the fates decide?
Is the gamble worth the gain?
Is the pleasure worth the pain?
Is the rainbow worth the rain?

I was sailing on the Sea of Love
With my dear one by my side
We found a message in a bottle,
Tossed upon that stormy tide.
It was the list of lover's questions,
The answers, no one ever hears,
Until they're drowning in the Sea of Love
In all those sad and salty tears.

Can you stand another broken heart?
Can you sing love's sad refrain?
Can you stop before the teardrops start?
Or are you gonna cry again?
Can you bet your heart and let it ride?
Live and love and let the fates decide?
Is the gamble worth the gain?
Is the pleasure worth the pain?
Is the rainbow worth the rain?

where are THEY ALL NOW?

I used to chase a milk truck
With an early set of friends
Down autumn streets and spring ravines,
We ran with swords and guns,
The ice was always bitter cold,
But life was never very old.
Where are they all now?
Can you tell me?
Were they really real?
Have you seen them?
Where are they all now?

Now the fat kid living down the street,
He always had the neatest toys
But the redwood fence around his house
Kept me and my friends at bay,
But he was good for fightin',
And that made life excitin'.
Where are they all now?
Can you tell me?
Were they really real?
Have you seen them?
Where are they all now?

Baseball games in backyards. Bow and arrow battles,
And tears we cried over dogs that died
And the sterling silver saddle,
On the pony at the county fair, that the guy you hated won
But you swallowed your pride just to get yourself a ride
When he got his treasure home.
Where are they all now?
Can you tell me?
Were they really real?
Have you seen them?
Where are they all now?

With bikes and trikes and kites and trees, we terrorized the town
But my old man always transferred and I had to start again.
My buddies they never came along. I turned the corner they
   were gone.
Now the faces so unclear to me and some don't come at all,
But voices vaguely cross the years—sometimes they come to tell
Of hiding in grandfather clocks, singing, winging sparrow hawks.
Where are they all now?
Can you tell me?
Were they really real?
Have you seen them?
Where are they all now?

YELLOW CAT

It's late December and the New Year's never coming,
Time passes slowly in a two-room walk-up flat.
The sun is silent;
There's a cold rain gonna come on.
No one to talk to but my lady's yellow cat.
The wind is whipping up the papers in the streets below.
I've got some books to read but seems they've all been read.
The clouds are crowded in a misty, drifting sky above.
I wish to hell I could remember what I said
I guess I could go walking
'Cause a cat's no good for talking to.
He don't know what I'm saying
And the rain is always playing on my mind.

Raindrops falling on the flowers in the window box,
Plastic roses that I planted yesterday.
I did not think they'd die so soon but they're all withered now;
Seems like everything I touch turns out that way.
Hollow echo of the raindrops falling on the roof
Like the voices of the shadows on the wall.
I watch the lightning licking clouds
And I hear the thunder roll.
Seems like years ago we never loved at all
I guess I could go walking
'Cause a cat's no good for talking to
He don't know what I'm saying
And the rain is always playing on my mind.

Streetlights sifting through the blinds that cover window panes,
Blends in softly
With the bare light overhead
And then together they run swiftly through my memory
An eerie image of a cold and empty bed.
One crystal wineglass on the table filled with scarlet stain
Stands alone and empty where there once were two.
The jug is silent on the cupboard by a broken plate.
The wine is gone my lady and so my love are you.
I guess I could go walking
'Cause a cat's no good for talking to
He don't know what I'm saying
And the rain is always playing on my mind.

NO REGRETS

It was a fatal day,
I took a look in her eyes.
They were green as they could be.
Let me tell you, fellows, so was I.
Time passed by and by
We tried to stay together.
You can take bets on it. Good help's hard to get,
'Less you got no regrets in your life.

Like the time I cried
When my daddy he died.
Such a common thing—the tears it brings
Can be hard to hide.
I hadn't seen my dad, and I was feelin' bad
Till I heard him whisper in the wind,
"Son, no need to fret. You owe me no debt.
Only have no regrets in your life."

My mama told me, "Son, don't make the same mistake twice."
I try to stay amused. I do what I want,
But I pay my prices.
At least that's what they say.
Sometimes I feel that way.
And I remember the folks that I met.
Well, I been out tradin' nickels for sets,
And I got no regrets in my life.

Saddest Man in Texas

You hear that moan?
You hear that pitiful cry?
That ain't no train,
It's just a fool goin' by.
He's making ready to leave,
A broken heart on his sleeve,
Saddest man in Texas!
He had no business going fooling around.
He made his bed and now he's 'bout to lay down.
He be sleeping alone; the boy, he's blue to the bone.
Saddest man in Texas!

Saddest man you ever saw
From Marfa clear to Arkansas,
Texline all the way to Texas City.
Saddest man from earth you know
From Paris, Rome, and Tokyo,
Saddest man from Conway clear to Twitty.
His walking papers took him right out the door.
She don't need him now,
She did not need him before.
From cactus down to the coast,
He's got the misery the most.
Saddest man in Texas!

Sadness is his occupation
Cries himself to dehydration
Saddest man that I can recall.
So morose it made him mean,
He got run out of Abilene
Now he can't go to happy at all.
Last time I seen the boy
He's down on his knees,
Hat in his hand and begging "Please, baby, please!"
Won't you just take a look
Right here in Guinness's book.
Saddest man in Texas!

Alice, Dallas to Palacious,
People crying "goodness gracious,"
Listen to that silly fool cry.
He damned near drowned in Amarillo,
Crying in his motel pillow,
Maybe someday he will run dry.
Check Mr. Webster for the right words to use.
There ain't no synonym for singing the blues.
In a maliferous mood, he's a lugubrious dude,
Saddest man in Texas!
From cactus down to the coast
He's got the miseries the most
Saddest man in Texas!

LOOKIN' FOR LOVE

Old dog sleeping in the sunshine, new dog barking at the door.
Dead dog lying by the roadside; he's not chasing cars anymore.
Bad dog hunting for a dog fight; the bird dog pointing at the gun
Devil dog running down the back road and the hot dog's lookin'
   for a bun.
Lookin' cause love ain't just a human condition.
Forgiveness is easier to get than permission.
Dogs and cats and birds and fishes,
Everybody's lookin' for love.

Fat cat standing with his hand out; hep cat juking on the floor.
Sail cat lying in the highway, and the cool cat's blowing five to four.
The tomcat's looking for a night out; the polecat's stinking
   up the place
The sad cat's sitting on the sofa; he's got tears rolling down his face.
He's cryin' cause love ain't just a human condition
Forgiveness is easier to get than permission
Dogs and cats and birds and fishes,
Everybody's lookin' for love.

Cat bird sittin' in the good seat; mockingbird singing me a song.
Big Bird singing on the TV and the baby bird's singing right along.
Jaybird naked as a newborn; the early bird's shouting out the news,
About the dove bird heading for the gumbo and the jail bird singin'
   the blues.
He's singin' cause love ain't just a human condition
Forgiveness is easier to get than permission
Dogs and cats and birds and fishes,
Everybody's lookin' for love.

Goldfish treasured in the fishbowl; cold fish giving you the hand.
Catfish feeding on the bottom; he's sucking up something from
   the sand.
Little fish hiding from the big fish; big fish looking for a meal.
Cod fish looking for the lost boys; I'm looking for my rod and
   my reel.
Love ain't just a human condition
Forgiveness is easier to get than permission
Dogs and cats and birds and fishes,
Everybody's lookin' for love!

LOVER'S WALTZ

You put your foot a little
Pedal-steel and fiddle, fillin' the floor.
They're dancin' brim to brim, he's holdin' her to him,
That's what dancin's for
They're a couple,
Every dance is taken,
They get so impatient when the band is breakin'
'Cause they want to be dancin' once more
She holds him close and his heart feels so glad,
She's the best girlfriend a boy ever had.
She thinks that he dances just like her dad
And they're dancin' to The Lover's Waltz.

She fed the kids their supper
Now she's fixin' up her hairdo just right.
He put the kids to bed,
Rememberin' what she said,
There's dancin' tonight.
The telephone is from the babysitter
Says she's not a comin', Mama made her quit 'cause
She's out too late dancin' last night.
So they'll do their dancin' on the back porch saloon
Kissin' and laughin' by the light of the moon.
All that they need is the time and the tune
And they're dancin' to The Lover's Waltz.

Mom and Poppa hug
They love to cut a rug when they get the chance.
Papa's gettin' older
He still loves to hold her close when they dance.
They look so happy dancin' elegantly
As he holds her lightly and he leads her gently
It's been a life-long romance.
He's still in love with that young country girl
She thinks that he's the best man in the world
She gives him a smile and he gives her a whirl
And they're dancin' to The Lover's Waltz.
We're dancin' to The Lover's Waltz.

Heroes

He was a gentleman from the South.
You should've seen him on his horse.
Him and that jughead they rode about.
It's been some years ago, of course.
There was a time when I loved him well
Though we had never passed a word.
But I witnessed some of the deeds that he'd done, son,
Wondrous stories I had heard.

There wasn't no one knew his name. He didn't mind,
They're all the same, if you're listenin'.
He had a lyric in his eyes,
They were the color of the skies,
And I wanted to go with him.
He was a Hero.

He helped the sodbuster save his farm,
When Bad Lee Rancher cut the fence.
He plugged a gunslinger, but he only shot him in the arm.
To heroes, killin' makes no sense.
His way with the ladies was kind of shy.
He usually shuffled in the dust.
A farmer's daughter she received a smile,
While his faithful horse received his trust.

Well, on his Appaloosa he could fill
The calaboose up in an evenin'.
He could catch the rustlers cold,
Save the gold and then be gone,
Before you knew that he was leavin'.
He was a hero.

We tried to get him to settle down,
As we gave thanks for what he'd done.
He single-handedly saved the town,
And then he rode off into the sunset.
He always seemed to be movin' on,
But of a hero's life I've learned,
He is a friend to depend upon,
If we're in trouble, he'll return.

Well, I'd like to buy a mule
And paint it white
And play the fool
And learn to draw quick.
Well, maybe he would let me
Ride beside him under western skies.
I'd be his sidekick.
He was a Hero.

IF I COULDN'T GET TO THE RIVER

If I couldn't get to the river
I reckon I would surely die.
The river can give a man reason to live
When the rest of the world says, "Why?"
If you're lookin' for somethin' that delivers
Come on give the river a try,
We can sit on the bank
Let our minds go blank
And let the rest of the world go by.

If I couldn't get to the canyon
I wouldn't have no place to go.
I love that ditch, Lord, I'd be rich
If I hadn't learned how to row that boat.
But she made me a true companion
One night 'neath the full moon's glow
Now the stars that shine
In the night are mine
As I rest by the old Bravo.

And if I can't get to my baby
There's gonna be hell to pay.
And I pity the man
Who makes his plan
To get in this ol' boy's way.
Ain't no ifs or ands or maybes
'Bout anything that I say.
She's my lovin' friend till the livin' end
Gonna see my baby today.

And if I can't get to the desert
You know the desert gonna come get me
It'll slip into town, all dusty and brown,
Come lookin' for the refugee.
Running with the desert is a pleasure
Always took the measure of me
And if you're lookin' around
And I can't be found
Well, the desert is where I'll be

Frontal Lobotomy

There must be a lotion, a potion,
A poultice that I could apply
A spell I could cast
Or a hex that would last
Or a pill I could buy.

I've been to brujos in shacks,
I've seen charlatan quacks
And I called on a wizard I knew
But the sorcerer said
I'd be better off dead,
Said there's nothing we wizards can do.
I'm gonna get me a frontal lobotomy,
Any old doctor will do
I'm gonna get me a frontal lobotomy,
Maybe then baby
I'll quit thinking 'bout you.
I'm gonna get me a bottle in front of me,
Any old whiskey will do.
I'm gonna get me a bottle in front of me,
Drink till the drinkin' and the thinkin' is through.
Thinkin' 'bout you is all that I do—
I'm goin' crazy baby thinkin' 'bout you.

You know, I talked to my preacher,
And my second grade teacher
And a prominent priest.
Well, I consulted the eight ball,
I talked to a shrink
And my aunt who's deceased.
Then I went to Bombay
To the Ashram to pray
And sit with the holy Hindu,
But the Baba just smiled,
Said "God loves you, my child,
But there's nothing us gurus can do!"

I'm gonna get me a frontal lobotomy,
Probably gonna take two.
I'm gonna get me a bottle in front of me,
Maybe then baby
I'll quit thinkin' 'bout you!

FAIREST OF FAIR WEATHER FRIENDS

He's the best of a bad situation
She's a good thing that comes to an end.
An impetuous infatuation
The kind of game nobody wins.
But he played a tune on her heartstrings
She put the words in his mouth.
He's always facin' the music
She's facin' the south.
And he wore a bad reputation
She was said to be wary of men
Now it's always a special occasion
For the fairest of fair weather friends.

They savor the taste of temptation
Longing to lie skin-to-skin
Seekin' that same old sensation
Been 'round since women and men
And he takes her dangerous places
Much to her sultry delight
And she takes him home for siesta
And deep in the night.
They continue without reservation
No need to lie or pretend
On a journey with no destination
They're the fairest of fair weather friends.

They meet for their brief assignation
He smiles when she welcomes him in
They part with no long lamentations
For they'll get together again
They share a passion for passion
And a glass of that sweet "by and by,"
They laugh at the luck of the lovers
And sometime they cry.

What began as a simple flirtation
Has now grown as wild as the wind.
It's a love with no great expectations
For the fairest of fair weather friends.

DINOSAUR BLUES

Me and my friends are getting long in the tooth
After three or four decades of seeking the truth
Trying to recover from misspent youth
And gradually giving in to knowledge

I know a picker who moved to Nepal
And another buddy's got a little shop in a mall
Some of my brothers ain't breathing at all
And others have given up privilege

But I'm still beating on my old guitar
Singing my songs in a smoky old bar
Hitching my wagon to a shooting star
And hoping that star don't fall

I'll keep picking as long as I can
But I don't want to die
Just a honky-tonk man
I'm just a buffalo singing the dinosaur blues

I was out last night, just me and a pard
Ain't nothing but a fool would drink that hard
You wind up sleeping in your buddy's front yard
And you wonder what to tell the little woman?

Me and the band's up all night long
We was passing the pipe and banging the gong
Trying to remember one of Van Zandt's songs
Something 'bout Mud and Gold and gamblin'

But I'm still walking down the lost highway
Doing what it takes to make my way
Knowing that I got a piper to pay
And hoping that I like the song

Maybe it'll be a ditty I know
I got people to see
And places to go
Just an old buffalo singing the dinosaur blues

I've been a lucky man all of my life
I got two great kids and a wonderful wife
Got a rosewood guitar and a very sharp knife
And I got a handy little knack for rhymin'

I been blessed with a voice that can sing
And a faith in the future and what it may bring
And change is the very most natural of things
And life is mostly attitude and timing

One of these days, well, I'll disappear
You'll look around and I won't be here
Don't worry, buddy, there's nothing to fear
I'm just going where the rivers flow

You can find me in a rubbery boat
Down in Mexico you can send me a note
Care of an old buffalo
Singing the dinosaur blues

FOOLS' GOLD

She glitters like fools' gold in a poor man's hand.
Beckons like a waterhole just a day's ride away.
The promise of a rainbow, risin' 'bove a summer storm,
The whistle of a freight come and haul my days away.
I never cared to be part of a crowd.
I never thought I'd be chasin' you out loud.

She's greener than Arkansas, lonely as the Trail of Tears.
Wants to see the things I saw, to stand behind my eyes.
She brought me an apple pie and a bottle of Arkansas wine.
The tears rollin' down her cheek will never wash away
   another good-bye.
I've got the memories. I had the time.
She was a melody. I supplied the rhyme.

Dear Darcy

Dear Darcy, here's a letter from a guitar,
He told me I should sing his song for you
And I should say it is from him;
He'd like to tell you where he's been.
But Daddy says it better when he sings.

Dear Darcy, how's your mama? Are you happy?
Can a guitar make a living where you are?
Well, your daddy's band and me,
We're just playing to be free.
But I still miss you listening to my strings.

Dear Darcy, can you see the wind blow by?
Covered up with snow like lookin' in a diamond's eye.
Dear Darcy, can you see the Northern lights?
Dear Darcy, is it really mostly night?
Are you all right?

There's a letter on the table from a guitar.
To a little girl who's gone four thousand miles,
And when she opens it she'll see
There's a postscript just from me
With all the love a letter's line can bring.

It'll say Dear Darcy
Do you miss me like I miss you?
Are you old enough to know the way I feel?
Am I man enough to see, how much in you there is of me?
And do you still believe your daddy's real?

Bears

There's some folks say there ain't no bears in Arkansas.
There's some folks never seen a bear at all.
Some folks say that bears go 'round eatin' babies raw.
Some folks got a bear across the hall.
There's some folks say that bears go 'round smellin' bad
And others say that a bear is honey sweet.
Some folks say "This bear's the best I ever had!"
There's some folks got a bear rug 'neath their feet.

Some folks drive the bears out of the wilderness.
Some to see a bear will pay a fee,
And me I just bear up to my bewildered best
And there's some folks even seen the bear in me.
So meet a bear and take him on out to lunch with you,
Even though your friends may stop and stare.
Just remember, that's a bear there in the bunch with you
And they just don't come no better than a bear!
No, they just don't come no better than a bear!

A LITTLE MORE HOLY

Let me feel my deliverance,
Won't you help me, Lord?
I'm a dangerous man!
With your blessed assistance, I might learn to be
A little more holy than I am,
Than I am . . . than I am . . .
Though I'm only a man
With my faith in Jesus, I might learn to be just
A little more holy than I am.

In my time of trouble,
Won't you help me, Lord?
I've done all that I can.
Won't you guide me gently through my misery
I want to be more holy than I am,
Than I am . . . than I am . . .
Though I'm only a man
With my faith in Jesus, I might learn to be just
A little more holy than I am.

Now, can you ease my madness?
Can you set me free?
Will you take me by the hand?
And guide me gently through my misery?
I want to be a little more holy than I am,
Than I am . . . than I am . . .
Though I'm only a man
With my faith in Jesus, I might learn to be just
A little more holy than I am.

BIRDS AND WOLVERINES

Birds don't get lost in the Everglades.
They follow the plan
That Mother Nature made
For each egg that's laid.
Some hatch out fine.
Some serve to dine the alligator.
Would it do for me and you
To be that true?

Hate don't exist in the wolverine.
He's just uncommonly natural mean,
But that's a wolverine scene.
His smell offends,
But he don't lie
About bein' friendly.
Could it be that you and me
Could be that free?

Bring to mind the buffalo.
Where did the passenger pigeon go?
Will the eagle be the next to die?
Make the national bird the common fly?
Why can't we live with the animals?
And be a boa constrictor's pal,
Or the great horned owl?
The common good
Is brotherhood
For the hooded cobra
And it should be that we
Could all be that good.

BLUE LINES ON WHITE LINEN

Blue lines on white linen is all that I write you,
And I pray will they find you,
And I hope they delight you
Blue lines on white linen is all that I write you,
How I wish I was with you tonight.

Would you dance at the wedding if I was a-askin'?
Maybe calling the parson,
To help us with our Sunday morn?
Would you dance at the wedding if I was a-askin'?
How I wish I was with you tonight.

At the end of the road there's a house with an orchard,
Where we could raise our kids.
An occasional orchid grows.
At the end of the road there's a house with an orchard.
How I wish I was with you tonight.

Copyright © 1976 Prophecy Publishing/BUG
Songwriter, Steven Fromholz (ASCAP)

PAINT WHAT?

Each and every endless day
For weeks that had become months,
He rose from his meager bed
Before the first glimmer of that
Glorious light he loved so well
And walked again through the silent,
Early morning to the chapel.

He there climbed the rickety scaffolding,
High into the sky inside the chapel,
To the place where he had
Yesterday stopped his labor
Because the light had faded,
And he had lain on his back, painting
Until he could no longer raise his right arm.

The glorious light
Had just touched the spot
Where he had left off yesterday,
When he arrived at the small pillow
Upon which he would lay his head
Until the light was gone
And he could no longer raise his right arm.

On his back, hour on hour,
Day after day, months into years.
One day I shall finish this, he thinks,
As he hears the huge doors of the chapel
Swing open in the sacred darkness below him.
He hears the voice of the Pope,
His employer, shouting from below,

"Michael,
What the hell are you doing up there?
I asked you to paint the chapel cistern!"
Michael shouts down to the Pope,
"May I finish this first?"
It shouldn't take more than 200 years,
Give or take.

Tree Prayer

Dear God,
Of all the things you've made
I am so grateful for the shade
Cast by this tree I sit beneath,
Which even cleans the air I breathe.
Birds live in trees,
They're often filled with chimpanzees,
And sloths, two-toed and threes,
Hang about in trees.

You can hang a hammock from them,
When they're hollow you can drum them,
And their leaves, they so become them,
In such wide varieties.
Elm and Birch and Maple
Whose syrup is a staple
On the buckwheat cakes I eat
Or with honey from Mesquite.

Texas has the most oak,
Scrub Oak, Pin Oak, Post Oak,
White Oak, Red Oak, Live Oak,
Dead Oak, which would have been all right oak,
If it wasn't for the blight,
That specialized in oak
Then the tree just ain't no good
'Cept to burn for firewood.

Another gift to us from trees
To warm the likes of yous and mees,
We all suffer from disease
From time-to-time, as do the trees.
There are trees I've never heard of,
Much less seen a bird of,
But I always shoot the sure dove
When it's sitting in a tree.

Perhaps it was there restin'
Or maybe it was nestin'
But I'm gonna put its breast in
My gumbo delicacy.
Thank You, Lord, for the Rosewood and Spruce
That the instrument makers put to such use
As violins, clarinets, and fine guitars,
Mandolins, castanets, and those strange sitars.

Apple and plums, peaches and pears,
And sometimes in trees you just might find bears.
Walnuts and Chestnuts and my favorite, Pecan,
These kinds of trees, a man could live on.
Cherries and Olives. All these treats for the palate,
From trees alone you can make a fruit salad.
Cradles and tables and beds for your slumber,
Easy to build if you've got the lumber.

Hickory for smoking.
Camp fires for poking.
White Pine for oars
And Cedar for drawers
And pianos made from Mahogany.
Paper for writing
The music delighting.
Without trees . . . there would be no symphony!

POETRY

What will you do when POETRY strikes?
Crawl under your desk, get on your knees.
Clasp your hands across the back of your neck
And tuck your head between your knees.
{and kiss your butt goodbye}
In a head on collision with POETRY, at any speed,
A seatbelt will do you no good.

When rowing your dory of story
Down the treacherous white water river that is the English language,
And you have safely stern-dropped the dangling participle
And you had no problem with splitting the infinitive,
And you are approaching one of the stretches of river
That makes no sense,
Even to the experienced boatman.

You know, the stretch where "womb," "comb," and "tomb"
   do not rhyme
But "rough fluff" and "enough stuff" do?
It is there, just below those terrible river rocks,
Left of "The Un-runable Hole of Rule and Order"
That lies the eddy of POETRY,
Which, when caught, offers a safe respite from the raging river.
But there is no place to camp.

POETRY is like an airplane landing.
Any poem you can walk away from . . . is a good one!

words

Words, when they begin to flow.
Can fall like tears.
Tears can be dried.

Words can stick to the roof of your mouth
Like creamy peanut butter.
Which can be wiped away with a finger.

Words can be lost like a Poet
In a strange city.
But a good map can find you.

Words can ring like a bell
And like a bell
You cannot un-ring them.

THE POETRY OF SPORT

The poetry of sport is in the motion,
Be it horses on the track
Or yachts upon the ocean.

The poetry of sport is in the heart,
Which gets you to a finish line
A long way from the start.

The poetry of sport is in the will,
That takes you outside yourself
To climb that last long hill.

The poetry of sport is in the gut,
Which keeps you in there fighting
While someone kicks your butt.

The poetry of sport is in the soul,
And it keeps you true and honest
As you strive to reach your goal.

THE 62ND BIRTHDAY

Today, measuring time as we know it,
I am sixty-two years old.
I look around me and I ask myself,
Hey Dummy, How did you ever get here?
I answer myself, Steven,
Everything you have ever done in your life,
Each good deed, every bad action,
Everyone whom you have met.

Every prayer, answered or unanswered.
Every chuckle and tear,
All you love and what little you fear,
And above all, The Grace of God
Brought you here today.
I believe the days are longer on Mars.
I wonder how old I would be
Were I born and reared on Mars?

THE BOXER

I will never listen to it again,
That song by Simon and Garfunkel.
Not that it's not a fine piece of work
And those two could sing the phone book.
It just takes me back
Way too far and way too fast.

Not to any special day
Or memorable event.
Unless you count your youth
As special and memorable.
I know mine certainly was
Or so I've read.

I AIN'T DROOLIN' OR DRAGGIN'

My friend said,
"Tell me about your stroke."
I said,
"I woke up the morning of
April 19th, 2003,
And could neither walk nor talk."
He asked,
"What did you do?"
I said,
"I mumbled and fell down!"

He said,
"And then?"
I said,
"I got up, mumbled something obscene,
And fell down again!"
I just kept getting up
And then, one day
I stopped falling down.
I list to port now,
And I talk with a limp . . .

. . . But I ain't droolin' or draggin'.

ODE TO an InDIana STaTe ParK HorSe

Oh, Joe!
I know that is your name
Because the the head wrangler
Told me so
And the tag on your rugged western saddle says "Joe."
When I touch you with my heels you go,
Not too fast, not too slow.
But you like to be second in line
Behind the lead horse who carries the guide
As you haul this poet on a one-hour ride.

Oh, Joe!
You one ton, four-legged, horsehide upholstered rocking chair,
You are one fortunate, equine rascal,
Spending your autumnal years
Walking along the gentle trails
Of Fort Ben State Park
Through the ash and the black walnut trees,
Startling the deer and wild turkey
And other scurrying critters
That go running at the sound of your foot fall.

I, Joe,
Sit astride your noble back
Surveying the morning light
Of the beautiful Indiana countryside
With my two poet compadres close behind,
Riding two of your capable stablemates
Yes, here I sit, feeling safe at last,
Knowing there is no better way
To see any countryside
Than from the back of a good horse.

And Joe,
You are a good horse.
Sure of foot,
Gentle of gait,
Patient with idiots,
Consistently,
Steadily, Joe.
Thanks for the ride.

MY BEST FRIEND

My best friend is a regular beast,
Bones and meat to him are a feast.
Each morning as day breaks in the east
He and I go walking.

I must open all his doors.
He has no thumbs, walks on all fours
We go outside and he does his chores
But I do all the talking.

He doesn't bitch and moan or pout
And of his love there is no doubt
He knows what his world's all about
You never hear him squawking.

The early morning is so fine
When I am his and he is mine
As the Texas sun begins to shine
And mockingbirds start mocking.

BEING HAD BY THE FUN

Oh, the places I've been
And the things I have done
Being had by the fun.

Back in the day, why we tried 'em all,
Had ourselves a ball
Being had by the fun.

I still have some friends
Who are facing dead ends
Being had by the fun.

Ah, the nights spent in jail
Waiting on bail
Being had by the fun.

Never counting the cost,
Hearts and livers we've lost
Being had by the fun.

Oh, the pall we have carried
For the friends we have buried
Who got had by the fun.

Oh, the things I have been
And the places I've done
Being had by the fun.

BOOTS

Fresh, new boots sit
In a cold bedroom
Next to old boots.
New boots are jealous
For they have soles solid
And smooth,
Without holes.

They cannot brag
About the wonderful sights
They've seen
And dirt they've eaten
From off the byways,
And sidewalks,
And cow paths.

After all these years

On display in the museum
At the Indianapolis 500 Speedway
Almost lost among the finest examples
Of 198 years of auto racing at the Brickyard,
Seemingly hidden among the
Alphas, Bugattis, Cobras, Ferarris, and Porsches,
Regally sits a 1927 Duesenberg,
Looking just like Angela Lansbury,
So good . . . after all these years

A COWBOY A-FOOT

There is nothing as sad or as sorry
As a cowboy when he's a-foot
No hoofs, no wheels, no wings,
Lord, how he hates to stay put.

His boots ain't made for walking.
They're built to slip in a stirrup.
A-foot, he feels like he's up to his butt
In grade A maple syrup.

But a cowboy horseback is a joyous,
Wondrous sight to behold.
Riding up old roads of wild flowers
Into sunsets of lapiz and gold.

A cowboy on wheels hauling something,
Perhaps it is only his ass.
He doesn't haul as far or as fast these days
Because of the price of gas.

A cowboy with wings is a flyer.
He says it's like being a sailor.
'Cause if you're in the sky or at sea, don't you see,
You cannot pull a horse trailer.

ISBN 978-0-87565-359-4

Steven Fromholz: New and Selected Poems
ISBN 978-0-87565-359-4
Case. $15.95
TCU Texas Poets Laureate Series